KEN MINYARD: THIRTY YEARS ON MORNING DRIVE AND THE FOXIFICATION OF TALK RADIO

Craig A. Horowitz

Table of Contents

Acknowledgments 6

Introduction 14

Chapter 1: Ken Minyard's Big Splash on LA's KABC 790 AM Radio 23

Chapter 2: Shock Radio Versus EGBOK 48

Chapter 3: From Ken & Bob to Ken & Barkley 59

Chapter 4: The Conservative Wave 75

Chapter 5: Minyard and Tilden 90

Chapter 6: Minyard and Minyard 99

Chapter 7: Minyard and Company 108

Chapter 8: The Retirement Party 120

Chapter 9: Beyond KABC 137

Postscript 150

ACKNOWLEDGMENTS

I moved to Los Angeles in August 1983 to go to UCLA Law School. I stayed with relatives of a then girlfriend in West Covina, California, about a 30 mile drive to UCLA in Westwood, California. They lent me a car and I drove from West Covina to Westwood at 7:00 a.m., not knowing anything about LA traffic. I put on the car radio and it was tuned to 790 KABC AM. I heard the Ken and Bob show, during my nearly two hour drive. Ken Minyard's wit, humor, intelligence and easy listening style immediately struck me. When I first interviewed Ken in August 2016 at The Grill on the Alley over lunch in Thousand Oaks, California, he asked me "why would you want to write a book about me?" Shocked by the question because I had a nervous morning getting ready to pitch a book to a radio icon, I told Ken "I had moved 3000 miles not knowing anyone. When I turned on the radio, I heard you. You were my first friend in LA."

This was true. As I listened to Ken over the years, I felt like part of his family. Many listeners held the same sentiment. His show made you feel good, regardless of the politics of the day.

I thank the many people who allowed me to interview them to recall the flavor of the shows and how Ken remained relevant in the "Shock Radio" era led by Howard Stern and the conservative wave started by Rush Limbaugh. I truly thank Ken for allowing me to do this project, not knowing my background or ability to pull this off. Knowing Ken considered himself a "Bobby Kennedy liberal," I brought to our first meeting my published book "The Legislative Legacy of Edward M. Kennedy: Eleven Milestones in Pursuit of Social Justice, 1965- 2007" and gave it to him. After talking about the book, I knew Ken would embrace the project. Even at that the first meeting Ken told me I had complete freedom to write anything about him - - good or bad.

When I asked Ken who he would like me to interview, he started with his children. This emphasizing to me the importance of family to a famous radio personality who had a "partier" reputation. I started with Rick Minyard, who Ken did a syndicated afternoon show with on a different radio station, KRLA from 1997 to 1999. Rick, a quarterback in high school and college, "quarterbacked" the many interviews necessary for this book, providing me necessary structure and enthusiasm. I next spoke to Kevin Minyard, Ken's second son, who passed away shortly after my interview. I also interviewed his daughter Dana Minyard. Each displayed their sense of pride for their father while giving me insight into Ken the radio figure on morning drive.

I also thank Jorge Jarrin, the traffic reporter but much more, who Ken made a huge part of his shows. Jorge, now a Spanish language broadcaster for the Los Angeles Dodgers, took a call from me at 9:00 p.m. after he landed in Colorado for a Dodger road series against the Rockies, and we spoke for two and a half hours even with him leaving the team bus and checking into the hotel. Ken suggested Jorge first after his family, and with good reason: both had such terrific and enduring memories to share.

Many others kindly interviewed with me. Jim Brown, a television writer who played a prominent role on the Ken and Bob Saturday Special, recalled with precision the ensemble cast and family feeling of the Ken and Bob Saturday Special in the 1970's and 1980's. Leon Kaplan, the "Motorman" with the longest running show on KABC, detailed his start on radio and interaction with Ken over the years. Rob Marinko, a current radio personality, with a decidedly conservative viewpoint, recalled the later part of Ken's KABC career from 1997-2004 when he began working on shows on the network.

Don Barrett, now retired, covered LA radio on LaRadio.com. Don kindly sent me a series of articles he wrote about Ken following his retirement. I also relied on an article he wrote in October 2017, commemorating the 13th anniversary of Ken's on the air retirement party.

I owe a great debt of gratitude to Doug McIntyre, the current host of KABC morning drive who took over for Ken in 2004. Doug and I met in person after one of his shows at the eclectic Culver Hotel. An architectural landmark, the setting proved able for Doug to ply me with Ken stories. More importantly, Doug went beyond expectations by putting me in touch with others who worked in the trenches of Ken's shows.

Through Doug, I interviewed Terri West, the Executive Producer of Ken and Company from 2001-2004. Given my interest in Ken's 2004 retirement party, aired live on October 15, 2004, Terri gave me Shelley Wagner's contact information, the Director of Marketing and Promotions of the show at the time, who did the nuts and bolts work for the final retirement program. She now works in the Marketing Department for the Dodgers.

I also interviewed Ken's delightful wife Jaqi. I appreciate her making me feel part of the Minyard family and her enthusiasm about this book.

I wish to thank Salina Dorado, a young woman who worked at our law firm Horowitz & Clayton while one of our Legal Assistants was on pregnancy leave. When her stint at the firm ended, I reached out to her to see if she would type this book and its many revisions. Salina, you stepped up to the plate and I am very grateful for your part in making this book work.

Finally, to my wife Cathy. Well, let's just say that since I started this book in August 2016, things did not go as we had hoped. But we have endured. You supported me and even held a book signing for my first book "Row 47," published in 2009, at your art gallery. You supported me in writing and getting a major publisher to publish my second book "The Legislative Legacy of Edward M. Kennedy" in 2014. You believed that a full time practicing lawyer, not an academic historian, could write a true history book. Now, on this book, when it has counted, you have encouraged me to move forward even though I had many good reasons to give up. I respect that you did not want me to give up and to do my best to put out this worthy book. I thank you from the bottom of my heart.

INTRODUCTION

The alarm clock goes off at 3:30 a.m. For most, this time of the morning means many hours of sleep before getting ready for the 9:00 a.m. to 5:00 p.m. work routine. Not for Los Angeles radio talk show host Ken Minyard. Working over 30 years from 5:00 a.m. to 9:00 a.m. on morning drive, Minyard kept hours that few of us imagine. What's more, he performed his craft for over 30 years (with one brief hiatus) better than anyone in the business.

While he endured management and format changes, Minyard's programs mixed humor along with the news of the day. Starting in 1973, at the age of 34 with his partner Bob Arthur, Minyard navigated listeners through Watergate, Nixon's resignation, The Jim Jones Massacre in Jonestown, the Reagan revolution, the Gulf War, the Rodney King beating, the OJ Simpson trial, the Monica Lewinsky scandal and numerous other historical events.

He did so both with serious coverage and humor. Coining the phrase EGBOK following the mass suicides (or murders) of 918 people in Jonestown in Guyana in November 1978, Minyard signed off each show assuring his listeners "Everything's Gonna be OK." Indeed, in 1986, Minyard received a surprise call from a 17-month hostage in Iran, recently released, who told the audience that EGBOK helped him get through his captivity.

Minyard retired from morning drive in 2004, announcing simply "It's been a great run, but I need to get some sleep."

Of course, Minyard's retirement stemmed from a number of factors. During his 17-year run with "Mr. News" Bob Arthur on the Ken & Bob Company, Minyard worked with many liberal talk show hosts on KABC, including Michael Jackson and Ira Fistell. By the time of his retirement, morning drive had shifted from the from the feel good approach of the Ken and Bob Company to what Minyard's now dubs as the "Foxication of talk radio."

Indeed, the Ken and Bob Company transformed talk radio. Minyard created a type of show never before aired. Assembling an ensemble cast, including sports recaps, lifestyle segments and political commentary, The Ken and Bob Company garnered #1 ratings for virtually 17 years straight ("Morning Zoo" teams popped up in every radio market in the country in subsequent years). In addition to his political acumen, Minyard added humor and flat out edgy skits. No show matched it. When Arthur retired in 1990, Minyard teamed up with long-term radio personality Roger Barkley in the Ken and Barkley show. The show maintained the format with Barkley playing the straight man just as Arthur did. The ratings remained competitive, even with the emergence of "shock radio" with Howard Stern. When the station fired Barkley, amid mildly sagging ratings, Minyard worked with then-edgy radio host Peter Tilden. Minyard himself got fired in 1999, only to return for a final stint with Dan Avey in 2001. By 2004, the station had turned decidedly conservative and Minyard felt it was time to retire.

Not many last in any business for over 30 years, much less in talk radio. Here, Minyard's career serves to chronicle the most important historical events from 1973 through 2004. While covering critical political topics, however, Minyard also weaved in jokes and lighter segments on the four-hour show. He made traffic reports fun by having an ongoing dialogue with Jorge Jarrin, who he nicknamed "Captain Jorge." With Jorge, he jumped out of an airplane at 11,000 feet along with a naked lady. Ken had Jorge train for the LA Marathon and the marathon was broadcast live with the early flip phone cell phones. Realizing the importance of colorectal screening, Minyard actually aired the events leading up to and following Jarrin's colonoscopy. He bantered with the show's sports reporter, Stu Nahan, calling Nahan's numerous gaffes his own language: "Nahaneese." He referred to the "Land of Nahahn" and would translate his sports reports into decipherable English. Trying to raise awareness on the dangers of drunk driving, Minyard did a show where he consumed alcohol throughout and while he got silly and funny he proved the point that drinking and driving presented a systemic problem.

In a 1994 LA Times interview, Minyard explained: "We never get bogged down. We find it very easy to switch gears between silly and serious. On any given day, in any half hour, in the conversation we can go from screwing around to getting into serious topics." While with Bob Arthur, the duo would yearly anoint a person a Starfish on the Redondo Beach Walk of Fame, akin to the Hollywood Walk of Fame. Minyard and Arthur in fact got their own star on Hollywood Boulevard, appropriately positioned directly in front of Fredericks of Hollywood.

Minyard's career did not proceed without controversy. When joining Arthur in 1993 for the morning drive "Ken & Bob Company," the fatherly Arthur often tempered the young, brash Minyard. Seventeen years later, when Arthur announced his retirement in 1990, he later claimed KABC fired him and it would not surprise him if Ken Minyard "orchestrated it." Minyard will tell the true story here.

Minyard also had a temper, although tame given today's talk radio daily norm. Minyard got into a famous argument with then show regular political analyst Murray Fromson, and Fromson never appeared on the show again. As his career proceeded, Minyard shifted from the brash host to one who mentored many radio personalities on to great success, including Tavis Smiley, Michael Reagan and KFI morning host Bill Handel.

Minyard also recounts here the strain he experienced with management and ownership changes, particularly when Disney bought KABC. And he pulls no punches. Refreshingly candid, Minyard describes the tug of war he experienced with Disney and program managers. With Disney searching for ratings and moving to a more conservative format, Disney failed to renew Minyard's contract in 1999, thus for the moment ending his then 26 year morning drive career.

Perhaps most importantly, during Minyard's career the entire landscape of talk radio changed. Once entertainment based with news coverage as an additional feature, talk radio first became "shock radio" with the likes of Howard Stern but then divisive and fervently right wing. Rush Limbaugh, Sean Hannity, Bill O'Reilly, Mark Levin and many others not only attacked Democrats but helped to fuel the current partisan divide our country now faces. Truth often secondary, this shift in morning drive and talk radio in many senses led to the ascendancy of the demagogue Donald Trump who became the Republican presidential nominee by appealing to hatred and fear mongering. Trump, shocking many, beat Hillary Clinton to become President. In his retirement, Minyard vocally opposes Trump and, not stifled by radio management, has made his liberal views well known on Facebook both through his own posts and on a page called Minyard & Minyard with his son Rick.

While we live in troubling times, no doubt if Minyard still did morning drive he would end each show with EGBOK. This book, through chronicling Minyard's career, explores how talk radio and morning drive evolved from such a feel good approach to the point today where, for the most part, it invites division and not the spirit of EGBOK.

CHAPTER 1

KEN MINYARD'S BIG SPLASH ON LA'S KABC 790 AM RADIO

Prior to television, most homes had a radio for entertainment. Families listened to variety shows hosted by such as Jack Benny. Few alive at the time do not remember the outcry created by Orson Welles' "War of the Worlds", aired on Sunday, October 30, 1938 as a part of a Halloween episode, which described an alien invasion by Martians.

By the early 1950s, television began its programming with Howdy Doody and other shows. Former radio hosts such as Jack Benny and many others took their craft from radio to TV. Many predicted the end of radio as seeing instead of listening captivated many Americans.

Radio adapted by replacing entertainment programs with shows of music interspersed by news and features. During the 1950s, automobile manufactures began offering car radios as standard accessories, and radio received a big boost as Americans listened to their car radios as they drove to and from work. Morning drive, though, had still not evolved.

Not surprisingly, major cities experienced the growth of morning drive. Starting as an evening show on WABC in New York, "Cousin Brucie" in the early 1960s wooed younger audiences with his music format. Don Imus' "Imus in the Morning" began on WABC in New York City and debuted nationally in 1973. While musical in nature, Imus began to integrate satire into his shows.

Meanwhile, 3,000 miles away, Los Angeles experienced a shift in emphasis on its morning radio show. Ken Minyard grew up in Oklahoma. He began his radio career as a high school freshman in McAlester Oklahoma doing a radio program. He continued his program and went to college at San Francisco State College. After stints at small radio stations in Northern California, Minyard moved to Minneapolis, Minnesota and did a radio show at WLOL. Ken had a spicy personal life. He married his wife Oma in 1958, had two children Rick and Kevin, and then got divorced. They both remarried, only to divorce and get married again. They had a third child Dana while in

Minneapolis. In the midst, Ken started at KABC in Los Angeles in November of 1969 doing a variety show in the afternoons.

An early picture of Ken, titled "Ken Minyard, Communicator," pictured a youthful Minyard on the grass with a woman stating:

> "This is a time for concern. Knowledge and experience change and renew themselves on an almost daily basis. It is difficult to find one's self and the role in society assigned us. Ken Minyard has built his program on concern for human relations. Open and honest, listeners trust and believe in Ken and listen to what he has to say."

With ratings not great and fearing his job, Minyard approached KABC management and asked for the opportunity to work on morning drive. KABC agreed and in 1973 he started broadcasting in the mornings with veteran Bob Arthur on a show called "Newstalk." The show already had an eccentric engineer who Minyard would call "Waco Pat." Minyard came on as the anchor to lighten things up and the show "The Ken and Bob Company" evolved from that. In the beginning, the show simply had Waco Pat, Bob, a financial contributor and a sports announcer. Promotions for the show on a TV commercial explained how "K" was for Ken, "A" was for "And", "B" was for Bob, and "C" was for Company, leading to KABC.

The show had no writers, and no rehearsals. Waco Pat's quiet drawl masked his dexterous handling of the fast paced show, pushing buttons, flipping switches, and juggling multiple remote feeds while ambushing guests with sound effects and voice tracks. Upon his death in 2004, Minyard commented: "I seldom set up any of Waco's bits and was as surprised as anyone with what he had come up with. He had a great sense of timing and the good sense to know what was appropriate and when to use it. Waco was a full partner in the show."

"Waco Pat" and Ken were close friends, even though during the show Ken would paint a picture of him as an illiterate Red-Neck from Texas. Far from it, Waco Pat had a true comedic sense and contributed to the wacky side of the program.

Minyard's vision back in 1973 in allowing and in fact encouraging "sidekicks" like Waco Paco to have free reign and banter with the hosts invented a new form of talk radio and morning drive, later copied everywhere with the "Morning Zoo" formats that prevail to this day. Now not simply news oriented, the Ken and Bob Company infused humor into previously dry news-oriented morning drive.

One legendary story involving Waco Pat occurred when Jimmy Carter came to the studio to be interviewed by Michael Jackson, whose award winning show followed the morning show. Ken had put a Waco Pat cut out over the urinal in the bathroom, with a hole to peep through. Carter "missed" and had urine stain the leg of his pants. Furious, Carter nonetheless did his interview with Jackson.

Minyard had no comedic background. He did not do comedy shops or anything of the sort. Asked about that recently, Minyard observed: "Me? Not in this lifetime. If you ever see me in a comedy club you'll know I had lost a big bet. I have never told jokes. The humor on our show was purely situational and organic."

Consider the need for this type of show as America went through the Watergate debacle. Unlike talk radio now, where every candidate's statement gets dissected and criticized in vitriolic fashion, Ken and Bob covered Watergate not with one sided commentary but with more phone calls and listener involvement. Truly talk radio. Obviously, significant revelations along the way culminating in Nixon's resignation received appropriate coverage. Certainly the show's lighter emphasis helped Southern California heal from the fractured events leading to Nixon's unprecedented resignation from the Presidency. Most importantly, Minyard created a bond with listeners. Many called in and Minyard both listened and engaged them, regardless of their viewpoint. His rapport with the audience no doubt lead to the unprecedented ratings the show received year after year. (17 straight years at #1 in LA).

Contrast how a liberal radio commentator like Minyard handled Watergate with how the dominant conservative talk radio show hosts address today every movement by first Obama and then by Hillary Clinton. Minyard calls this the "Foxification" of talk radio-- and with good reason. It never occurred to Minyard in 1973-74 to push a political agenda. Rather he commented on the news that Arthur reported in what many term as a "polite" way. Minyard viewed his role "as being a disc jockey but instead of playing music we played the news." Arthur had already established himself as a news anchor on LA radio and TV. Arthur, openly reluctant at first, got on board with the format as its success grew.

And its format—a light view of the news reported with humorous bits—did not exist before. Bob would open the show, bellowing "Gooooood Morning." The show with Ken had spontaneity as his son

Rick said, "Ken knew when to kill the bit." Ken would arrive, pre-internet, with newspapers in hand and a highlighter. He had scissors where he would clip news articles he felt worthy of discussion, and set them aside for an appropriate time to discuss. Soon, an ensemble began to form on the show. Ciji Ware joined the show in the mid 1970's as a lifestyle reporter. Reminiscing on Bob Arthur after his death, Ware wrote: "Bob and I worked together on KABC's #1 drive time radio program for more than 15 years and he was the glue that kept the enterprise together that long. What a total sweetheart he was: a true gentleman, and kind to this 'newcomer'—the only woman on the show for at least a decade."

Ware's tribute to Arthur came on the second anniversary of his death in 1979. Likely a slight to Ken, Minyard recalls an on air fight between them. The topic: women in the military was new at the time and Minyard commented that he felt certain physical differences between men and women needed to be considered. Ware bristled and called Minyard a sexist. Well, this created a "Cold War" between the two until Minyard got home from the show one morning only to find a bouquet of flowers with a card from Ciji saying, "Sorry Ken." Minyard came to work the next morning all smiles only to learn that Ware had received a bouquet of flowers at her home with a note: "Sorry Ciji- Ken." George Green the station manager at the time, tired of the feud, sent them both flowers in the spirit of EGBOK.

Indeed, Minyard coined the name EGBOK, "Everything is Gonna be OK" in response to the Jonestown Massacre in 1978. Jim Jones formed a cult, called the "People's Temple," an American pseudo-religious organization in northeastern Guyana. 909 Americans died from Cyanide poisoning, an event Jones termed "revolutionary suicide." Minyard was driving home after the exhausting show where the details came out and remembered what a friend of his once said – "tragedy happens every day somewhere but there is no reason to cancel your bowling game because of an earthquake in Peru." In other words, "keep the right perspective. "Everything is Gonna be OK." For some reason, as he pulled into his driveway, Minyard thought of the phrase EGBOK. It became the signature feature of the show. Signing off each day at 9:00 a.m. with EGBOK, listeners from 1973 to 2000 to the Ken and Bob Company had a unique but comforting experience each morning. Many listeners woke up at 5:00 a.m. to hear the entire show, not wanting to miss the various reports from contributors and the banter between Ken and Bob.

While Ciji Ware filled the lifestyle slot on the Ken and Bob Company, Notre Dame Graduate and former NBA Player Tommy Hawkins became the sports anchor on the # 1 AM morning show. Known as "The Hawk," Minyard frequently quipped about Hawkins' active night life while Hawkins gave his sports summaries. Hawkins did nothing to disabuse the audience of his Playboy image and active bachelor life. In fact, he fueled the image with frequent segments with Minyard on the subject. Hawkins later had a prominent role with the Dodgers, but always remained a friend.

On politics, the Ken and Bob Company presented all viewpoints. Minyard, a liberal, had cordial interplay with right wing commentator Bruce Herschensohn. Herschensohn appeared regularly, commenting on the politics of the day. One can scarcely imagine any current conservative talk show host allowing a liberal a frequent spot on a top rated show. But Minyard's vision of talk radio embraced a reasoned discussion from all viewpoints. Indeed, Minyard's friendship with Herschensohn led to a scandal during Bruce's run for Senate against Barbara Boxer in 1992. Then off the air, Minyard with his wife had dinner with Herschensohn and his female companion and the four then embarked to Hollywood on Sunset Boulevard to "The Seventh Veil," a nude strip club. Word of their visit leaked out the Thursday before the Tuesday election. While Herschensohn would have lost anyway, he worsened things by holding a press conference against Minyard's advice that simply accentuated this truly unimportant event. Rick Minyard, Ken's oldest son who later would pair with his father on a syndicated afternoon show, had a key role in Herschensohn's previous campaign in 1986 for the seat being vacated by Alan Cranston, which was won by Boxer.

Unknown to many listeners, these contributors did so remotely, from their homes. Although it sounded like it, they did not come to the studio. Ken acted as the "conductor," creating a flow to the show that it made it seem he and his guests were in your living room.

And sex was never off limits on the show. Minyard brought in a soft porn actress Edie Williams to come to the studio while Bob Arthur was reading the news. She wore a fur coat which she proceeded to remove and then she was stark naked. She sat right next to Arthur. Arthur, showing what a professional he was, never broke stride until the end of his segment. At that point, Arthur and Minyard had some words but in the end Arthur knew the skit simply increased the show's popularity.

This was tame, by comparison, to "Shock Radio" what would soon emerge with Howard Stern. Minyard conceived a feature called "Lust News," comprised of oddball stories in the news that had some sexual angle. Minyard describes it now as "tame stuff" but back then was ground breaking. The segment would include stories with a sexual twist, and mostly humorous with much left to the listener's imagination. Many listeners looked forward to that segment and once again the Ken and Bob Company had a feature unmatched by any competitor. This broadcast was not so far removed in time from the Dick Van Dyke show where he and Mary Tyler Moore slept in separate twin beds on the famous sitcom "The Dick and Van Dyke Show." America may not have been ready in the early 1960's for sexual innuendo but Minyard introduced it to radio. Minyard also featured a segment called "Nude Phone Calls," where listeners purportedly called while nude. The point was humor and quite innocent but it stirred a good response and ratings. Ken played up the calls, leading listeners to imagine what the callers looked like naked, while no doubt many simply called while driving to work. He also had a segment filled with humor called "stuff most people don't know about."

One gag meant to lighten things up during the 1979 gas crisis occurred in the town of Harmony in Northern California, population 17. Minyard went through the little town and met the people who owned the town. It had a post office, a pottery shop and a café. Ken and Bob talked about Harmony on the show and decided to do an old fashioned fair with kissing booths, food, and a cow chip throwing contest. They also had a float and got Bob Barker of TV game show fame to announce the parade. The floats took up all of the only street so the floats stood still and people walked by them. A stationary parade.

Ken and Bob broadcasted the event on a Saturday and had about 3000 people attend. Since Harmony is up past Morro Bay and about 30 miles north of San Luis Obispo, some gas stations along the way agreed to stay open for the Ken and Bob Company listeners. A couple who listened regularly had their wedding that day. Bob Arthur gave away the bride and Minyard was best man! Quite an event to help people cope with the gas shortage and staggering inflation. The later part of the Carter years, filled with negativity and with rampant inflation and gas rationing, could not stifle the spirit of EGBOK.

The remote events captured the family comradery of the show. Listeners joined Ken and Bob on a trip to Ireland for St. Patrick's Day and the duo had a wedding shower in London for Princess Di. They broadcast from Hong Kong, Hawaii, Germany, Australia, Israel, Austria and London. They also did live shows from the Academy Awards, Dodger Stadium and the Los Angeles Mission. For years, KABC was the flagship station for the Dodgers, and it was an annual tradition, and obligation to the Dodger contract, to broadcast for a week from Vero Beach, Florida – the spring training site for the Dodgers. While initially fun, this became one of Minyard's least favorite weeks of work. Ken's wife Jaqi recalls the Australia trip. They were in a cab with Bob and George Green, the General Manager of KABC at the time. Ken and Green got into a shouting match about the broadcast, and Ken asked the cab to stop in the middle of Sydney traffic. Ken and Jaqi got out and found their way back to the hotel.

Indeed, while fiery at times, during the 17 year run of the Ken & Bob Company, Minyard spearheaded the #1 rated radio program in LA. Minyard's innovation departed from staid news reporting and traffic reports. The show, never pre-scripted, involved many impromptu segments, often presented on a hit or miss basis. Minyard's genius was to realize that in the aftermath of Watergate and in the midst of the Cold War, many Americans worried daily. His show diffused these tensions.

Ken's son, Rick Minyard, who would later team up with his father on the syndicated afternoon drive show Minyard & Minyard, describes his father as a "Bobby Kennedy liberal." While one detected his liberal views on his shows, they were subtle. Rob Marinko, a current conservative KABC personality stated that, "even after I knew of

Ken's politics, I remained a listener. The show simply engaged the audience."

Jim Brown, who worked for the Los Angeles Times as its radio columnist, met Ken in the early years of the Ken and Bob Company. Brown went on to become a successful television writer for Dynasty and day time dramas. He also became a close friend of Ken and became part of the "Ken and Bob Saturday Special." Aired on Saturday mornings from 6:00 a.m. to 10:00 a.m., the show actually got recorded Wednesdays after the morning show ended at 9:00 a.m.

The show had a lighter pace, and according to Brown, had more of a family feel to it. So imagine waking up for Saturday morning not to infomercials as now, but to a tight group of friends making jokes and spinning yarns. Jim would have a segment on TV shows or whatever the week would bring.

After the taping, Ken, Jim and others would have lunch at the Moustache Café on Melrose, and spend the afternoon over drinks. It became a special bonding time for those committed to bring KABC the best entertainment possible. Ken orchestrated it, but contributors like Jim made it work.

And they all socialized. The Ken and Bob Team were not just Monday to Friday workers, all had deep friendships. Jim Brown describes the "Ken and Bob Saturday Special as a "convergence of friends." The chemistry of that pre-taped show remains unmatched.

Another regular on the Ken and Bob Saturday Special, Leon Kaplan, talks with great fondness about Ken in general and the Saturday show. Kaplan began his radio career at KABC doing segments about once a month on Elmer Dills' show on Sunday mornings. At that time, Dills did a regular, general show, not his later acclaimed restaurant show. From there, Kaplan, an expert in cars, airplanes, and boats, anything with a motor got invited by Minyard to be a regular on the Ken and Bob Saturday Special.

Kaplan credits Minyard with "teaching me more about radio than anyone. "With such expertise especially on automobiles, Ken instilled on Kaplan to "keep it simple." Back in the beginning, Kaplan had a seriousness to him and Minyard "taught me how to loosen up a bit." Ken even helped Kaplan name his show when he became a regular host on Sunday mornings. Originally called "The Motorized World of Leon Kaplan," Minyard convinced Leon to go by the name "Motorman." The name has stuck with Kaplan for over three decades.

The two also had fun after taping the Ken and Bob Saturday Special on Wednesdays. Leon recalls a particular Wednesday when after taping the show, Ken wanted to have lunch in Catalina. Kaplan had a race boat in Marina del Rey. A normal tourist cruise takes an hour and a half to two hours. Kaplan got the boat to 100 miles per hour and made it to Catalina in 35 minutes. This led Ken to refer to Kaplan as "flat out Leon."

Aside from the fun, Kaplan remembers Ken for his willingness to help him get his real start on radio. "Ken had the number 1 radio show in Los Angeles," Kaplan recalls, "and here I was new at it but he could care less." "Everything I learned in radio was from Ken Minyard," Kaplan said in an interview. "Minyard had a wit to him," Kaplan observed, "and he encouraged me to let loose on my show." In fact, the two bonded so much that for a time, KABC bought a bus and Leon did the driving while Ken and Bob did remote broadcasts from the back of the bus and hundreds of people would greet them at various announced stops. Jim Brown and Leon Kaplan certainly more than assisted in the Ken and Bob Company's long run as Number 1.

The Ken & Bob Company would further evolve before Bob Arthur's departure in 1990. One critical facet involved traffic reports with Jorge Jarrin emerging on the show in 1985. Ken had a concept.

Why not ease Jorge, a young prospect, in all aspects of the show. This idea created an entire new dynamic to the show. Minyard soon dubbed Jarrin as "Captain Jorge" in "Jet Copter 790" and involved him in a myriad of topics on the show. Jarrin got in the helicopter each morning at 5:00 a.m. and nonetheless engaged an audience. The son of legendary Spanish radio icon Jaime Jarrin, who broadcasted Dodger games, Jorge soon developed a persona of his own, assisted by Ken. Jarrin credits Minyard with his success:

> "This is the man I owe the most to in my radio career. He was the ringmaster, and at times the ringleader, depending on what mischief he was up to for the benefit of his loyal radio audience. Astute, intelligent, irascible, and perceptive, he was mining ratings long before there was Howard Stern, Mark and Brian, Kevin and Bean or Rush Limbaugh. It was by far the best time I ever had on radio and a great pleasure to be part of the Ken and Bob Company, which later

gave way to the equally successful Ken and Barkley Show on AM radio KABC."

Jarrin almost did not get the job. KABC had already decided on a female Jet Copter reporter. But program manager George Green heard Jarrin on Sports Talk with Tommy Hawkins when Jorge had been a member of the Los Angeles 1984 Olympics Committee and tracked him down through his father Jamie Jarrin, the Spanish broadcaster for the Dodgers. He fit perfectly. As Jarrin says: "You couldn't have taken yourself too seriously on the show or you were a goner."

It was the type of interplay that endeared the audience to the Ken & Bob Company, making it the highest rated show for its 17 year run. Jorge also covered news events, from fires to freeway chases. He had a gift for such reporting, and contributed much to morning drive on KABC. He was honored by the Associated Press for his coverage of the 1992 Los Angeles Rodney King riots.

Jorge and Ken's relationship endured even more years but in the early years Ken really transformed the role of a bland traffic reporter. Today, traffic broadcasts are short and laden with commercial sponsors. The traffic folks hardly interact with the radio hosts. Jarrin, to the contrary, was a centerpiece of the Ken and Bob Company. Jarrin credits Minyard with his career success, and today they remain close as Jarrin now announces Spanish Dodger broadcasts with his dad.

Minyard's blend of an ensemble cast along with the broadcasting of serious news revolutionized talk radio. Many tried to replicate Minyard's approach but his #1 AM radio rating for 17 years attests to the success of his approach. While Minyard incorporated sexual innuendo into his segments, he soon would be challenged by Howard Stern and "Shock Radio." As will be shown, Minyard was up for the challenge.

CHAPTER 2
SHOCK RADIO VERSUS EGBOK

As the Ken and Bob Company solidified itself in LA morning drive, a new radio star emerged. Howard Stern moved to the prime time morning slot in February 1986. His New York talk show became syndicated in August 1986. Heard around the country, Stern provided a provocative and decidedly different radio program, centered around strippers and sex. Stern also entered the TV market with his shock show theme. Stern hosted a pay per view event "Howard Sterns's Negligée and Underpants party" in February 1986. Stern joked about drugs being used backstage but nothing came of it.

Still, Stern had created a new brand of radio, catapulting him to the highest rated morning radio show in the New York market. Meanwhile, 3000 miles away, Minyard continued his number 1 rated "The Ken and Bob Company."

The Ken and Bob Company continued its dominance in Los Angeles morning drive even with Shock Radio penetrating the market. The entrance of youthful, traffic reporter Jorge Jarrin certainly helped

Minyard's cause. He used Jarrin in so many different ways than any traffic reporter before.

Jarrin, the son of now hall of fame Spanish Broadcaster Jaime Jarrin, was born in Ecuador. Many assumed he was Mexican, but he came from South America. He and his family moved to Los Angeles when he was a year old in 1955.

Jorge studied theater arts at Pepperdine graduating in 1979. He learned to perform but soon realized he was targeted for Chicano casting roles, which he did not like. He went into sales and editing but got laid off. In the meantime, he married his wife Maggie.

Jarrin served on the Olympics organizing committee in 1984 and as a public relations officer for KABC. In 1985, KABC wanted an on air traffic reporter for morning drive. Then station manager George Green tracked down Jorge and interviewed him. Jorge did not fly and thought he would not get the job. He did. Jarrin spent two weeks learning the trade in Dallas, Texas, although he did not fly himself at any point. Ironically he started his job at KABC on September 16, 1985- Mexican Independence Day.

Jorge soon learned that the pilots of the helicopter leaving at 5:00 a.m. often had troubling staying awake. So Jarrin soon got his training to fly. And Minyard soon realized he had a rare talent.

Jorge became Ken's favorite target for a stunt. Minyard, not doing the Howard Stern routine of live radio accompanied by TV shows of nude women often tantalizing Stern with sexual talk, had his offbeat "Lust News." But then Ken came up with an audacious idea. He wanted Jorge to jump naked from a plane, along with Ken who would wear a jumpsuit, with a woman who jumped naked from the plane. Of course, they needed to have someone to jump with Ken to accompany him to ensure their safety. Jorge's jumping partner was Vinnie. Minyard kept prodding Jorge to jump naked. But Jorge said he would only do it with boxer shorts on.

So Ken jumped with his jumping trainer partner to help, and Jorge leapt from the plane at 11,000 feet with Vinnie. Jarrin describes the jump, broadcast on the radio, in intense detail. According to Jarrin, he expected the parachute to deploy almost immediately. Instead, the jump was a free fall from 11,000 to 3000 feet, which took between 45 seconds to a minute. Jorge was hyperventilating and felt like he was going to throw up. Once the parachutes came, Jorge found relief but in comedic fashion. So relieved, Jorge on the air explained "Oh, Vinnie, Vinnie, this is great!." Jarrin describes it as sounding on the air as the "longest orgasm." A Fox 11 camera crew also caught the jump and landing.

Indeed, the format created by Minyard withstood the "Shock Radio" trend. Interviewed in the Los Angeles Times and asked how he fared so well against his competition such as Howard Stern and Mark and Brian on Los Angeles' KLOS, Minyard said: "People sort of take us for granted. I understand we have been around a long time but…if you look back, you'll see that over the past years we've been far and away the dominant show in the market. After all that time and with all the (competition), we have weathered the storm. Yes, it's frustrating for people not to acknowledge that. We went through (the success of such other Los Angeles morning personalities as) Rick Dees, we went through Mark and Brian, and Jay Thomas had his day, and so on. And we have stayed right there in the hunt. Big time…Everybody said, 'Radio is going to this trend: Shock jocks!' Everyone hasn't gone that way. The other approach works too."

Asked how the advent of shock radio altered his show, Minyard responded: "The good side of it is it allows us to go further than we used to be able to go. You don't have to second guess yourself on where the line is. Because wherever the line is, we don't even approach it."

Minyard also pulled no punches about Stern: "The thing I object to about Stern is how cruelty has come to be equated with humor and I don't find it very funny." Every morning, according to Minyard, Stern had a bunch of women undressing. Minyard explained: "Doesn't he do that every morning? If you hear that on a daily basis, how long can you find it funny? Is that really creative? Does it make him a humorist?" Asked how Minyard viewed the change in talk radio, he replied: "First of all, I don't think of us being talk radio. We're a morning show... Talk radio is getting to be a not very nice thing. Because on some stations it seems they'll do anything to outdo the other guy. They don't seem to have a commitment to any real idea, but to do anything that will get some attention. So they're just whores. And it didn't used to be that way."

Minyard also prided himself on appealing to an intelligent and older audience: "I also don't like the trend at some stations to put people down because they're over 55 years old. They're trying desperately to appeal to this young, hip audience. There is nothing young and hip about you if you're constantly saying how young and hip you are." Minyard termed the "Shock Radio" trend as the "tabloidization of the media in general."

Minyard, never once to mince words, in 1989 said that his listeners, unlike those of his rivals, can actually spell their names. This drew some ire from a Los Angeles Times reader, who wrote: "Well Ken, I can spell my name and I can even teach those who can't, all despite the fact that I don't listen to your show."

To some extent, Minyard understates the edge to his show. While plainly appealing to an educated group, Minyard's on and off the air antics did in fact appeal to a younger audience. Jarrin, in glowing terms, refers to Minyard as a "rascal." Minyard always searched for skits and concepts that would engage the listeners. Shortly after Jarrin began, the show aired on Columbus Day. Jarrin had a gift for doing fake accents, so Minyard had Jarrin do all of his traffic reports that day "in Italian." On St Patrick's Day, he used an Irish accent. Jarrin recollected that he would "do anything for that sake of the show." This sometimes irked Jarrin's wife, who told Jarrin "you're not allowed to come out to play with that little Kenny Minyard.

And Minyard did like to "play" on and off the air. His daughter Dana describes how Minyard could charm almost everyone. She recalls that Minyard had a Porsche when she grew up in his house in Chatsworth, California. The home was quite a hike to the station on La Cienega in Culver City, California, a good 35-40 miles. Minyard would leave at the last minute, and drive 80 miles per hour down the freeway. One early morning a police officer pulled him over for speeding. Minyard explained who he was and why he had driven so fast. The officer not only gave Minyard a pass, but would often wave to him in the mornings as Minyard sped by.

Jarrin also recalls that Minyard could throw a good party. He had purchased a vacation home up in Lake Arrowhead, California, a small town 2 hours outside of Los Angeles and at an elevation of 5,500 feet. Lake Arrowhead gets snow in the winter. According to Jarrin, Minyard was very generous and "simply liked to have fun." Many weekends were enjoyed in those years by the morning team.

Yet he resisted the Shock Radio movement. Minyard certainly recognized that Stern had tapped on a certain market: "The things people on the extreme edge of broadcasting do open doors for others, for better or worse." Minyard noted in an LA Times interview in 1992:

> "I certainly listen but I'm no longer sensationalized by hearing him talk about body parts or scatological things. I don't really find it funny. It seems to be the same thing all the time. He's got some babe in there and he's asking her to take her top off and it just got boring to me. I would guess that other people, as they get over puberty, will feel the same way."

Just as Minyard had to adapt and innovate in the fare of Shock Radio, an even broader challenge would emerge as well. While Howard Stern continued to titillate and talk about sex with his wife, a wave of right wing conservatives, led by Rush Limbaugh, would soon begin to dominate radio airwaves. At the same time, Minyard would begin a transition from the Ken & Bob Company to the Ken & Barkley Company.

CHAPTER 3
FROM KEN & BOB TO KEN & BARKLEY

No show in morning drive, or in any day part, had a better run than The Ken & Bob Company. From 1973 to 1990, the show routinely ranked first in its time slot. Through those years, the show evolved into a multi-faceted four hour program with regular cast members, impromptu skits and serious news coverage. As Jarrin says, Minyard "was the ringmaster." The show also had a Ken and Bob Saturday special taped on Wednesday's after the morning show. With an even lighter touch, the show focused on weekend events and lifestyle issues. In addition, for a short time KABC expanded the show from 5:00 am to 10:00 am, until Ken told management he simply could not do the extra hour. The duo got a star on the Hollywood walk of fame, as shown in the pictures on the preceding pages.

By 1989, Arthur was approaching 70. Not only that, but his voice over time became increasingly hoarse, making it difficult for him to read the news. Ratings began to slip some, and Minyard sensed management might want to make a change.

Arthur plainly wished to stay and had no intentions of retiring. In 1982, KABC ran a commercial with "Isabel," one of only supposedly 12 people who did not listen to the Ken & Bob Company. Bob Arthur appeared youthful in the clip, with his deep voice resonating. Just seven years later, his voice had all but left him. In addition, the show -- facing shock radio star Howard Stern and newly syndicated arch conservative Rush Limbaugh -- had serious ratings challenges. Management placed most of its attention on the 25-54 year old demographic, which is what advertisers target.

By no means did Minyard engineer Arthur's ouster. But Minyard candidly admits he did go to management and advised that if a change were to occur, he would like to team with Roger Barkley, who had spent 25 years on the Lohman and Barkley radio show before an abrupt and bitter break up.

Signs of the end of the Ken & Bob era subtly emerged. Barkley would sit in for Arthur when his voice was hoarse. Soon enough,

KABC announced that Arthur was leaving the show to help set up a group of care homes for Alzheimer's disease patients in Long Beach, California. He stated at the time he needed to devote his full energy to the project, citing motivated local opposition to the care homes.

The final Ken and Bob Company broadcast took place at the Century Plaza Hotel in Century City with thousands of listeners dropping by to say goodbye to Arthur. Arthur said in an interview before the finale that "it really hasn't been that much different this week because we've been so busy concentrating on the show." But deep down Arthur bore resentment which would later come out.

Minyard at the time described the 17 year partnership with Arthur as follows:

> "It definitely is like a marriage. But when you're together six hours a day for 17 years, you spend more time than married couples. What's remarkable is that

we've had maybe half a dozen arguments during all those years."

One argument stemmed from an April's fool's joke Arthur played on Minyard on air. For all of Arthur's seriousness he knew how to pull a prank. Arthur and the other company members decided to disagree with everything Minyard said on the show that day. Minyard would introduce a commercial and the wrong commercial would be played. Arthur also managed to let listeners in on the prank. "He became so upset that he kicked a wastebasket across the room and stormed out," Arthur recalled. "He exploded."

In explaining the success of the Ken and Bob Company, Minyard attributed it to their professionalism and optimistic spirit. At the time, Minyard said: "People could trust us to pass along the news, the good and bad but we would also help them keep things in perspective." Arthur explained their popularity and longevity in a different way:

"I've heard it said that it was like eaves- dropping on a poker game where the stakes were not very high."

Arthur did end his final show on September 14, 1990 with the phrase EGBOK. But everything was not okay with Arthur. He did not retire, and claimed in an October 4, 1991 Los Angeles Times Article that he was fired by KABC, Arthur maintained that he was forced out by KABC management due to his age and his friend and on air partner of 17 years, Ken Minyard, "orchestrated it."

Arthur departed in September 1990, after 23 years with KABC. In a letter written to the Los Angeles Times in response to a story about the one year anniversary of the Ken and Barkley Company, Arthur wrote: "Retirement, hell! I was fired." Arthur slammed Minyard:

> "Ken Minyard did not learn of my plans to retire—he orchestrated them. It was all well planned by Ken

and (KABC General Manager George) Green. Though a series of maneuvers it all came to pass."

Green and Minyard strongly denied the allegations at the time, expressing surprise and characterizing Arthur's letter as "lashing out." Green commented in the article:

> "I'm disappointed he would do this after a year. I don't know what he is going to benefit from all this. He wasn't being ousted because of his age. It had nothing to do with his age. Bob departed, orchestrated by him, with his acknowledgment. He contributed a lot to this radio station. It was a very classy retirement and I don't want to say anything a year later. He is seeing the success of the Ken and Barkley Company."

Green's last sentence certainly was an unnecessary dig at Arthur, given his body of work at KABC. Minyard at the time distanced himself from the situation. In a telephone interview, Minyard told the Los Angeles Times:

> "Where does he get that information? That's obviously speculation on his part. That's what I was afraid of. Bob is bitter and lashing out and wanting to blame other people. Believe me, the decision was not mine. It was between George (Green) and him".

Arthur, an award winning newsman, advised at the time that wanted to set the record straight. According to Arthur, he had gone along with the retirement story to fulfill an agreement he made with KABC to ensure he recovered severance pay.

Arthur described a rather blatant conversation with Green. "First, he started off asking how old I was," Arthur said at the time. "He said, see Bob, you're 71 now aren't you." Arthur replied "No, I am 69." Then Green told Arthur, according to Arthur, "I wanted to tell you

Bob, we are terminating your contract as of December 31, 1990." Arthur told the LA Times: "They are lucky I haven't filed an age discrimination claim against them."

Arthur then described that he participated in a "retirement charade." Arthur claimed Green blamed him for sagging ratings, even though the Ken and Bob Company retained a top three ranking. Arthur noted: "I didn't say anything at the time (of leaving the station) because I didn't feel I wanted to cause any difficulty. It was the tenor of the quotes that compelled me to say there's at least more than one side of the story."

Green continued to accuse Arthur that his remarks at the one year anniversary of the Ken and Barkley Show demonstrated Arthur harbored jealousy at how well the new show had done. Arthur, in a strong rebuke, replied:

> "I'm not angry. I am not seeking revenge at all. I would have done that on January 2, not a year after I

left the air. It was only the comments (about the new show's ratings success and younger demographics) that prompted me to say this is going a bit too far. The implication was (that) I'm gone, so they got a younger audience. That with my demise the young ones are flocking over, making me responsible for the ratings drop. If (Green) had let sleeping dogs lie and had not made it appear that I was responsible for the program going downhill, I would have let it go because I've let everything go for a year. But these were downright lies."

But Arthur did feel betrayed by Minyard. He described his retirement party as "a very elaborate charade." Arthur further noted that "people turned out by the thousands and I was grateful for their words. They were generous in their praise and generous in their applause and I think they were kind. It was most appreciated, the loyalty of the fans."

Arthur did not have such kind words for KABC management. "But the ulterior motive (of KABC management) was not to make me look good as much as it was it was to make the station look good and dull any criticism that might come up…It was show business, look how they milked that." Arthur said he felt betrayed by Minyard: "I considered Ken, if not a best friend, a very good friend. We had shared confidences, we had both gone through raising our kids together. We'd gone on vacations together. We saw each other socially. There were never any indication that this sort of thing would happen."

Minyard commented at the time that he was saddened by Arthur's remarks:

> "Bob and I had a lot of good years. If, in fact, there was unpleasantness when he left, it wasn't with me. But it's not uncommon for a person to not be working some place and start charging other people with all

kinds of things…It's too bad we have to get into this. We certainly had a nice run. As to our personal relationship, what difference does it make? I don't want to respond to that. It's not the stuff that needs to be paraded through the newspapers."

Unfortunately Ken and Bob did go through a divorce. And, ironically, both went through martial divorces during their time together on the show. Ken met his wife Jaqi, who worked at the station, in the late 1980's after getting divorced from his wife Oma a second time. The two married in 1991 after Ken and Bob's "divorce". And it does seem clear that Arthur took his departure very hard.

Meanwhile, the new show Ken and Barkley launched.

Roger Barkley, grew up in Iowa and moved to Los Angeles to work at KLAC in 1961. He became the program director of KLAC, and hired Al Lohman to do the morning show. When KLAC was bought by Metromedia in 1961 the new owners began to search for a two person morning program. Roger said at the time: "We figured we were all going to be fired so Al and I thought perhaps we should do the morning show as a team; this way we could buy some time to look for another job." For the next 25 years, Barkley played the straight man, interviewer and narrator as Lohman voiced different characters.

Barkley tired of the format, involving playing various tunes including The Eagles and Springsteen, and Lohman increasingly arriving late at the show. He resigned and viewed his role in the Ken and Barkley Company as a new start.

Minyard welcomed Barkley, stating at the time: "I was never really worried. I had a tremendous sense that Roger should be the guy to step in." Barkley at the time said that he viewed Ken as the lead and relished the opportunity to be his straight man and side kick.

The show subtly changed. Minyard introduced an early morning segment with Barkley doing a spot called "In Your Papers," summarizing the morning news. According to Minyard "In Your Papers was our way of framing the day's news in short form and saving the listeners from having to read it themselves."

The duo also organized a Christmas show in 1991. The LA Times reported:

> "On the Road to Christmas: As Santa points his sleigh homeward to the North Pole, the team of KABC's Talkradio's Ken and Barkley Company will climb in a van to spread Christmas cheer to some families in Los Angeles and Orange County. Ken Minyard, Roger Barkley and the rest of the Program's regulars will go door to door, singing Christmas carols and delivering gifts, while broadcasting today's show from 5-9 am. Others in the KABC family include

Waco Pat Patryla, Stu Nahan, Ciji Ware and Barbara Esensten."

This human touch distinguished the Ken and Barkley Company from shock radio and the conservative movement led by Rush Limbaugh. Interviewed in 1994 by the L.A Times, Barkley noted: "Where talk radio is really valuable is in the times of crisis. It provides a real outlet for people who have emotions they want to express to somebody. The Northridge earthquake is a really good example of that." Minyard quipped in the same interview: "We have a disaster planning wing of the Ken and Barkley Company that tries to create various disasters in order to build ratings."

While Barkley explained the value of the human approach of the show, Minyard knew that in the radio business, ultimately ratings mattered. And the Ken and Barkley Company, while not departing significantly from the Ken and Bob format, kept up its ratings.. On August 21, 1994, L.A. Times staff writer Gloria Puig wrote in the

Entertainment Section: "This may surprise you, but Ken Minyard and Roger Barkley have the top rated 5-9 a.m. show in Southern California. In a world increasingly dominated by Howard Stern and his ilk, how do they do it?"

The answer, of course, rested in the variety of news, humor and an excellent ensemble that kept listeners engaged. Minyard and Barkley developed an excellent rapport, and the audience liked it. Soon enough, the challenge to the show came not only from Shock Radio, but from the conservative wave led by Rush Limbaugh.

CHAPTER 4

THE CONSERVATIVE WAVE

Having moved seamlessly from the Ken and Bob Company to the Ken and Barkley Company, Minyard had not only to deal with Shock Radio but the conservative right talk radio that became the dominant form of talk radio since the abandonment of The Fairness Doctrine in 1987. The Fairness Doctrine had required radio stations to present contrasting political viewpoints. The Federal Communications Commission (FCC) stopped enforcing the rule and talk radio stations could now present totally conservative viewpoints.

To be sure, Ken's station KABC in Los Angeles did not shy away from conservative talk. For years before, its overnight host Ray Briem presented conservative views mixed with the paranormal. The station also hired Larry Elder, a conservative African American who cut his teeth covering the OJ Simpson trial but who later displayed a right wing agenda, while calling himself a libertarian. (Elder would later change his political affiliation to Republican).

Then, Rush Limbaugh emerged. As noted in the Wall Street journal, "Ronald Reagan tore down this wall (The Fairness Doctrine) in 1987... and Rush Limbaugh was the first to proclaim himself liberated" from what he conceived as liberal dominated talk radio. Limbaugh began a national radio show at WABC in New York in 1988. Limbaugh completely supported the Gulf War and ridiculed peace activists. He wanted the Bush administration to overthrow Sadaam Hussein. He vehemently opposed the election of Bill Clinton and tore into every aspect of his political agenda. Clinton, a moderate Governor from Arkansas, represented to Limbaugh and his listeners a dangerous left wing radical who would convert America to socialism.

Meanwhile, Ken and Barkley kept with their format, tweaking it to appeal to a younger audience. "They have a special synergy," said KABC General Manager George Green. "Ken is like the bad boy and Roger is like Mr. Righteous, with a naughty feeling underneath!" As the show progressed in the 1990's, the program developed segments such as "stuff most people don't know about," "weirdities in the news," and "cheap and sleazy gossip."

At this time, Geraldo Rivera had written a tell all book. The show moved a bit to that direction. According to General Manager George Green, "We would never have done the Geraldo thing before. They step up to the line a little more these days and we have to pull them back." Yet, the show truly did not have a gossip aura. It really continued the ensemble approach to a diverse show that emphasized news, humor, and the lighter shade of things.

For those of us alive during the Gulf War, we have searing memories of bombing of Iraq and scud missiles launched to Israel. Broadcast every night on the Ted Koppel show "Nightline" on ABC, these were serious times. The Ken and Barkley show did not shy away from reporting these events, but interspersed their lighter segments to make the mornings easier. In some respects, this radio style trumped the relentless Limbaugh attacks, which wore down listeners.

Ken tried to change the image of the show, but was rebuked by management. Minyard initially resisted the Shock radio and conservative attack: "I never tried to combat any kind of surge. I just tried to do a good and entertaining show. I was not a crusader." Minyard continues: "Our show was always about a satirical take on the culture. Roger and I started to refer to ourselves as The Bad Boys of Morning Radio." Management recoiled and the duo stayed fairly conventional. Ken regrets the constraints stating: "Sadly you just can't stay conventional white bread forever. Until you are regressing. We continued OK but we could have done much better."

In many senses, though, Ken and Barkley did just fine with its wide ranging format. While adding humorous segments, the duo also covered politics. In fact, Ken and Barkley broadcasted during Bill Clinton's inauguration on January 11, 1993 live from Washington, D.C. Minyard and Barkley "were in the big scaffolding thing that was up alongside the Capital building where all the photographers and broadcasters were." In a subsequent November 4, 1994 radio interview with Clinton on the morning show, Minyard quipped to the President: "And you waved at us, I think. That was very nice of you."

The Clinton interview illustrates both the humorous and serious side of the show. To start the segment, Ken and Barkley began with the music Clinton had played on the saxophone on the then popular late night television program "The Arsenio Hall Show." After introducing the President and with Minyard commenting on the low unemployment figures, Clinton responded: "Now I am supposed to say, Great Show aren't I?" Minyard continued:

"Q. Oh yes, let's start from the beginning. Ladies and Gentlemen, the President of the United States

A. The President: Great show, Ken and Barkley.

Q. Oh. Thank you so much.

The President: I've got my lines down."

After beginning the interview of the sitting President with frivolity, Ken turned to a serious interview. Minyard asked Clinton whether he had underestimated how tough being President was, with reality setting in that he was dealing with Haiti and the Middle East. Clinton responded: "I think I underestimated a couple of things. First of all, the difficulty of having to manage both a domestic and foreign policy at the same time when both needed so much change, because we need to be strong at home and strong abroad and fighting for good jobs and strong families and safe streets at home and fighting for greater security and freedom and democracy abroad, that is something I underestimated."

The interview continued with Clinton listing his accomplishments in the short time he had been President, such as the Brady bill, the ban on assault weapons, and the economic plan. With time running out on the short interview, Minyard shifted gears again, quipping "But we also wanted some time to tackle the issue of Don Imus versus Ken and Barkley, but we will do that another time." President Clinton responded: "You guys are doing pretty well, I think."

Indeed, Ken and Barkley in 1994, continued to do quite well. On a political note, traffic reporter Jorge Jarrin in 1992 received awards for his coverage of the Rodney King riots. Flying in Jetcopter 790, Jarrin painted a vivid scene for listeners in the aftermath of the controversial verdict. Meanwhile, back in the studio Ken and Barkley reported the breaking news. Together, with Jarrin describing the horrific, vivid picture of the looting, fires and carnage, Ken and Barkley reported the listener's reactions. Compelling radio permeated those mornings. And even with these searing events and a fractured Los Angeles, Ken and Barkley continued to reinforce EGBOK each morning during the tragic events of the verdict and its aftermath.

The duo also covered the OJ Simpson trial in 1995, just like all other media. But the Simpson trial did not dominate the show. TV shows and radio programs easily provided ample coverage. So Ken and Barkley continued their ensemble cast and skits, once again to keep listeners from dwelling on the sensational trail.

Interviewed in the Fall of 1994 edition of KABC's "Let's Talk" magazine, Ken and Roger expressed mutual admiration for each other.

Minyard stated about Barkley: "What I do like most about Roger is his timing. The man has great instincts. He knows when to argue a point, to set up a joke, or just let me make a fool of myself. Barkley remarked: "Yes, I certainly consider Ken a close friend. A good example of our friendship is when we spent a week together in Europe with our wives. We were together most of the time working, dining, and sightseeing and we never tired of each other. Barkley continued: "What I really admire about Ken is his show business instinct. He's cutting edge. Ken has a good sense of when to push the limits to be competitive."

By 1994, The Ken and Barkley Company had quite the ensemble. Waco Pat remained the "crack" Ken and Barkley Company engineer. Ted Payne delivered the news, even with interruptions from Ken and Roger. Stu Nahan continued doing sports, if the listeners could understand his "Nahaneese." Jorge Jarrin remain the unwilling "stunt-man" and kept listeners out of traffic jams. He had the assistance of "Dr. Roadmap," who expertly gave listeners alternative routes when traffic clogged the freeways. Bruce Herschensohn provided a conservative voice, with a sense of humor. Gloria Alred made sure the "boys" remembered the female point of view. Tavis Smiley became the official Ken and Barkley "Generation X" contributor.

As with the Ken and Bob Saturday Special, the station had The Ken and Barkley Saturday Special. "Motorman" Leon Kaplan kept doing his car segments. Barbara Esensten provided lifestyle reporting. Jim Brown knew what was hot around town, and did television reviews. Margo Kauffman added a unique and humorous voice to the Saturday show. Dr. Alan Selner, dubbed by Ken as the "podiatrist to the stars," served as a fitness expert. And finally, Sondra Lowell, the "tap dancing news lady," recapped the week's news while tap dancing and singing. Doug McIntyre, who would succeed Ken in 2004 upon his retirement, stated in an interview that he thought "Ken was at his best with Roger Barkley," even though Ken achieved his fame with Bob Arthur.

One contributor, Ken Roycroft-Davis, Assistant Editor of England's newspaper "The Sun," initially was invited in 1991 to discuss a story he had printed in his newspaper about Princess Diana's steamy phone conversation with her former lover. After a few more informative reports, Chris was dubbed "The Official Ken and Barkley European Correspondent." Chris accepted Ken and Roger's offer to visit Los Angeles. When asked about the difference between Brits and Angelenos, he responded: "That's easy. Everyone's much more friendly here. People are more open and enthusiastic- particularly if you have a baby with you. In England, we're reserved and shy." The Ken and Barkley Company broadcast live from the Hard Rock Café to commemorate the last day of his visit in Los Angeles. Another Ken and Barkley character, Michael "The Irishman" Jackman, shared a limerick to give Roycroft Davis his proper send off.

Soon, though, with Shock Radio and the conservative wave of Rush Limbaugh and his ilk, Minyard detected that management wanted to make a change. He got wind of a plan to fire Barkley in 1995, but Ken fought for him. Indeed, their ratings still were good.

By 1996, the Walt Disney Co. owned KABC in Los Angeles. Acquired by Disney in early May 1996, Disney installed Maureen Lesourd as President of the station. While the Ken and Barkley Company's ratings had only dropped slightly, Disney made the decision, according to the LA Times, to bring in "the younger, more frenetically funny Peter Tilden, who had been the morning show host on sister station KMPC-AM (710)."

The change brought forth a number of reactions. To begin, Barkley did not get a sendoff of party such as Arthur did. Minyard announced the change to the dismay of a preponderance of callers. Calling from her car in the 8:00 a.m. hour, a woman who identified herself as Claire said if Barkley "surfaces" elsewhere, "that's where she is going." Minyard pleaded, according to the LA Times, "Don't be a bitter." Earlier, Bernice from Santa Monica said she was heartbroken… I can't believe you would allow it to happen… It could happen to you, couldn't it?" Minyard acknowledged that it could. Jean from Hollywood said she was "not happy with Disney." Brian from La Habra said that if KABC wants a new sound, it might be looking for new listeners. "I'll be looking around. KABC stabbed their listeners in the back."

Dave Cooke, KABC operations manager and program director, downplayed the listener discontent, stating: "Roger is one of those marvelous individuals but not only a great broadcaster but also a true gentlemen. He will be missed by all of us at KABC, but the time has come for a significant change in the direction of the morning show. Ken and Peter are two of the funniest, most intelligent quick-witted and talented people in the industry." Minyard told the LA Times: "He was upset. There were no two ways about it… But Roger understands, like we all do, these things happen… We had a great six years together. On the other hand I look forward to what I think will be a new challenge."

As for the new show with Tilden, Minyard said "Peter is the funniest guy I know. He constantly makes me laugh. My challenge is going to keep up with Peter's hyper pace." Minyard stated that he and Tilden "will combine strengths. Both of us, I hope, are funny. My interests are more in the direction of political and topic- oriented, and Peter's is more features and entertainment." Explaining the change Cooke commented: "We felt that it was time for a show with a faster pace, just a more exciting, entertaining show. And I am absolutely confident the guys can give us that."

Tragically, Barkley died just a year later at 61 after a short bout with pancreatic cancer. Former President and General Manager of KABC George Greene told the LA Times: "He will be missed by the industry and especially by the community, who adored Roger Barkley. This has nothing to do with ratings. Forget about the show biz bull—Roger will always stand in my mind as one of the greatest talents and one of the greatest human beings I ever worked with." Minyard observed: "He was such a gentleman. Will Rogers never met a man he didn't like, I never met anyone who didn't like Roger... He was a wonderful professional." Sadly, Barkely held resentment against Ken, having the belief that Ken agreed in ousting him. In truth, Ken fought for Roger Barkley's job for a year. Management would not relent, so focused on the younger demographic as they were. Ken's son Rick reports that one of Ken's the saddest moments came when he was advised by a colleague not to go to Barkley's funeral.

With now Ken and Bob and Ken and Barkley gone, Minyard would face his new challenge teaming up with Peter Tilden, on the show called Minyard and Tilden.

CHAPTER 5

MINYARD AND TILDEN

In September 1996, Peter Tilden replaced Roger Barkley to become Ken Minyard's latest sidekick. The L.A. Times described Tilden at the time as "frenetically funny." Minyard well understood Tilden's humor could bring a new edge to the show.

Tilden, a Philadelphia native, left KFI's morning drive with Tracy Miller to join Minyard. Tilden said at the time that he intended to complement Minyard and that Minyard remained the lead. However, not a news guys like Arthur and Barkley, Tilden did not fit easily in the role. Minyard later reflected: "We were a mismatch. Peter was used to commanding a show with his humor and I had been the one who had supplied humor to my shows for the prior 23 years."

Tilden, when interviewed, denied a strain with Minyard. Tilden stated that he "loved Ken and learned a lot from him." Like Minyard, Ken's son Rick Minyard who would later do a syndicated afternoon drive show with his father on KRLA, had a morning show in Modesto at the time. When KABC Management decided to let go of Roger

Barkley, Rick hosted weekend practice sessions in his modest studio as Ken and KABC Management, particularly George Green, decided who would next join Ken as a co-host. Green wanted to appeal to more of the 25 year to 54 year old demographic. Green felt that Barkley had not stayed current and the show needed more of an edge. In addition to Tilden, Ken wanted very much to convince Gean "Bean" Baxter to join the show. His show Kevin and Bean on KROQ debuted in 1990. Bean had an interest but contractual obligations precluded him from joining KABC. Rick Minyard recalls well the tape auditions, which would occur on Saturdays in Modesto. "It was exhausting actually," Rick Minyard said. "With Peter, the practice sessions had a frantic pace." Ken, at the time, felt he would prefer Bean due to the chemistry during the practice sessions, but KABC chose Tilden to join Ken in the new Minyard and Tilden show.

Ken reflects: "I was absolutely opposed to it at first... I said Peter and I are both number one guys. Neither of us fill the role of a sidekick very well. It just did not make any sense." In a LA Radio Magazine in an article by Don Barrett Ken recalled:

> "Peter was very enthusiastic about it and I told him exactly, exactly what I felt. I told him there's no question that he was the funniest guy in the building but I said what's funny at the water cooler could and sustaining it for over a four hour period are two different things. I said I thought his humor should be framed. You just can't keep topping a funny joke with another funny joke. You know you've gotta have a beginning, a middle, and end then move on, giving people to catch their breath."

KABC management went forward with the program. As to Minyard's observation, Ken told Barrett at the time: "Peter agreed with me and so we decided to give it a shot. As it turns out I think my initial reservations were correct. I don't think it was an ego problem, I think it was a style problem." Dave Cooke, who had become the Program Manager, made the suggestion that "one segment Ken is the lead guy, Peter is the straight man and the next segment Peter's the lead guy." Ken found the idea absurd, and the show did not proceed that way. Thinking back on the show, Ken remarked: "It was unfortunate… I've got to tell you that I got a lot emails and they say Minyard and Tilden was my best show. I don't agree and by no means do I mean that as a reflection on Peter, who is a great talent."

The two also had fun. Tilden did not drink but related when interviewed that "when challenged, I could drink." Ken set up an evening at a Santa Monica restaurant. Peter recalls having about 14 tequilas, which Ken beat. Peter threw up all night but Ken made it to the show the next morning and did it solo. Peter enjoyed hanging out with Ken. He recalls his "party house" in Lake Arrowhead. "Ken had a full bar like a restaurant." Peter quipped, "me at home I have some beer in the refrigerator that is ten years old." Peter's affection for Ken came out loud and clear during his interview.

However, on the air duo did not mesh. Whereas Ken did a lot of his show by feel, Tilden produced his segments beforehand. He also had a writer at the show daily who would feed him a joke to conclude his segments on the show. Ken did prepare. A voracious reader, after getting home from the 5 am-9 am show, he would nap and liked to take a bath. There, he would read to stay topical and fresh.

Peter, desperately seeking to have a fast pace, simply tried too hard. According to Rick Minyard, Tilden ended every segment with a punch line. It seemed forced and maybe a bit contrived. Ken describes the show as his least favorite time on the radio. Ken did not dislike Peter. He just did not like the product the show produced. It came to the point where during many of Tilden's segments, Ken would either leave the studio or take a "cat nap." Unlike in earlier years when the show traveled with listeners, that did not happen in the Minyard and Tilden era. The two, according to Rick Minyard, "were not buddies."

With Tilden having a comedy writer producing segments, the show lost its spontaneity and that disturbed Ken. Ken had always been the "funster," while Bob and Barkely played the straight man. This dynamic ceased to exist on Minyard and Tilden.

As a whole, KABC presented this type of show to deal with part of the shock radio wave brought on by Howard Stern. Peter knew celebrities and part of the show catered to them. He could name drop and tell tales of his interactions with Hollywood types. Ken, despite all his fame and his star on the Hollywood walk of fame, did not cater to and join in on Hollywood events. In this sense, the growing dissatisfaction Ken felt for the show becomes more understandable.

By this time, Bill Sommers, President and General Manager of KABC, had chosen to cancel the show after just two years. In November 1998, just two years after the show began, Disney chose not to renew Ken's contract. Ken had a 7-figure contract and the decision had much to do with saving money. Compared by these days AM radio ratings, Minyard and Tilden's 3.5% rating looks impressive in retrospect. Despite being dispatched after more than a quarter century on KABC morning drive, Minyard said at the time: "they were very, very generous about it. I told him (Sommers) when we spoke I wanted to have everything very amicable." Despite that comment, Ken had enough and chose to depart that Friday. Tilden commented at the time "especially since Ken wasn't going to be there, I didn't want to be there." I had a great time. Honestly and truly. I'm looking forward to doing my own thing now."

Rumors abound that KABC offered Tilden the show but he declined. Having listened to the final shows, it seems like Tilden took the high road and did not accept a replacement spot. Tilden went on to do Southern music on FM and returned to KABC in various roles, currently a 10:00 a.m. to 12:00 p.m. slot.

KABC originally replaced Minyard with John and Ken from KFI. But Minyard had other plans in place. He soon surfaced on KRLA began an afternoon drive syndicated show with his son Rick, still in Modesto, called Minyard and Minyard. While the thought of the syndicators had "liberal" Ken fighting against his supposedly "conservative" son Rick, the show took a decidedly different turn.

CHAPTER 6
MINYARD AND MINYARD

When KABC did not renew Ken's contract, he had no intention of "retiring." Ken's son Rick had a morning show in Modesto and Stockton. Ken had bought two restaurants in Modesto in 1990 and Rick moved up to Central California. Rick had taken broadcasting classes and got his introduction to radio on KYOS in Merced, California before moving to KFIV in Modesto, where he hosted the mornings and served as Program Director. That show, syndicated also at KJOY in Stockton, lasted for over five years. Rick emulated much of what his father had done. He took the show on the road and broadcasted from Washington, D.C. He had an ensemble of sorts, with Bruce Herschensohn contributing with phone in reports.

Rick actually led Herschensohn's Senate campaign in 1986. He organized Bruce's appearances and backed him as the candidate to replace the retiring Alan Cranston. While Herschensohn and Ken stood at opposite sides on political spectrum they became and remained close friends.

With Rick running the campaign and later viewed as a conservative, after Ken left KABC, KRLA in LA approached them about doing an afternoon drive show from 3:00- 7:00p.m. with the focus on them arguing politically as father and son. The show was syndicated to over 95 stations through Talk Radio Network out of Oregon.

When the show began, the duo did the show remotely, with Rick in Modesto and Ken in his studio in his Hollywood Hills home. The issue driven show involved political debate and interviews with the newsmakers of the day. One thing Ken and Rick disagreed about was Bill Clinton. Ken supported him while Rick did not like Clinton. The station seized on this, describing Ken as a Bobby Kennedy liberal (which he was) and Rick as "passionate Libertarian." Conservative Broadcast Network.com described the new show as having "sparks for as they bring eye opening, morning like sizzle to both sides of issues on the homeward side of week days."

The show began on January 4, 1999. For the first week, the duo broadcast the show from the Museum Of Radio and Television in Beverly Hills. "It'll be the type of show I've done my entire career," Ken Minyard explained at the time. "There'll be issue oriented talk but it won't be just talk about politics. And humor will play a big part." Fred Shuster of the Daily News reported in a December 24, 1998 article titled "L.A Life" that "the younger Minyard said he differs from his father politically." According to Shuster, Rick said, "I'm what you call conservative, and dad is a liberal."

In fact, the dichotomy expressed did not truly exist. "We agreed on more issues than not," Rick Minyard said in a recent interview. Rick feels that the division in political viewpoint KRLA and the syndicator attempted to portray was contrived.

Still, in touting the show at its origin Ken told LA Times reporter Judith Michaelson: "We thought it would be fun to do a show together, particularly in that our views on political things are quite different. It would provide a diverse set of opinions from hosts and yet obviously we get along, love each other, and that might be instructive too." A very keen observation particularly in this time of huge political divide and unprecedented partisanship.

Interviewed on December 31, 2008 before the show first aired on January 4, 2009, Ken continued:

> "It's going to be a morning show in the afternoon. I want it to be a complete show. I want it like we used to do it on KABC. For people going home in the afternoon, it's not much different from those getting up in the morning. They want to be informed, and they want a few laughs. We'll also discuss politics but I don't want to get bogged down in that. For the most part, our show is going to be a magazine. It's going to cover politics, sports, feature stories, outrageous stories, interviews with newsmakers, and interviews with

authors. We're going to develop regular contributions, we're going to have movie reviews…You're going to be able to keep up with what happens in the world that day . . . the serious stuff and the not so serious, but it's certainly going to be current."

The show began right as the impeachment debate regarding Bill Clinton dominated the news. Rick chimed in: "I say impeach him." Ken retorted, "You say convict." Ken reminded "he's already been impeached. I say it's the Republican's version of coup d' etat… There's a Senator today—Robert Bennett of Utah- who says he'd be for censure as long as the president was publicly and solemnly humiliated. I thought that said a world about what Republicans are up to." Rick then noted "We're both opposed to censure but for different reasons. It's just a meaningless gesture, it does not mean a darn thing—particularly because the President is so anxious to be censured."

This type of discourse strongly suggests that, at the outset, the Minyard's intended to voice different political views in a nonconfrontational way. Asked about New Years Resolutions, Ken quipped: "How about a diversity of views on Talk Radio? That'd be a quality change, don't you think? I know a new afternoon show on January 4th that plans to provide that."

Ken had promised contributions to the show like in the Ken and Bob days but it did not quite pan out. According to Rick Minyard, however, he does not remember any true contributors like in the Ken and Bob days. Rick also feels that the syndicators "pushed them in an unnatural direction." Although Ken and Rick disagreed on Bill Clinton, they did not disagree on much else.

While the show did well, KRLA did not. It became the landing place for major former KABC talent, such as Michael Jackson and Ira Fistell. But the station overall never did improve its ratings. In the summer of 2000, KRLA dropped the Minyard and Minyard show. At the time KRLA had "stayed put in 32nd place" in the ratings. In a searing letter to the editor of the LA Times, Rick Minyard wrote on July 29, 2000:

> "The assertion by KRLA- AM program director. Ron Escarlega to The Times that Minyard and Minyard was steadily losing listeners is quite simply false (Morning Report, July 14). In fact, from the winter 2000 Arbitron survey to the spring, "M&M" gained in every key age demographic: 12 plus, 25- to 54 and 35-64.
>
> An examination of the Arbitron book would show that "M&M" had the largest book-to-book percentage increase in share (75%) of any part of the station's schedule, the largest actual cumulative audience of any KRLA show next to Michael Jackson and a larger audience share than Don Imus or Gordon Liddy.

Consider all of this in light of the fact that we were preempted by the audio feed of CBS local television news during our last hour.

Ken Minyard and I respect the decision by KRLA to program its stations with infomercials if it chooses. What we object to it is the apparent attempt to use us as some sort of scapegoat for the station's overall dismal place in the LA market."

Problems preceded the show's termination with the syndicators TRN Talk Radio Network, and litigation ensued. Ken and Rick cannot comment about the suit due to a confidential settlement.

While Rick turned to a successful business career, Ken was not yet done with radio, He soon began his final stint on KABC, teaming up with veteran news anchor Dan Avey, in a morning drive show titled Minyard and Company.

CHAPTER 7
MINYARD AND COMPANY

In November 2001, KABC brought back Ken Minyard and paired him with veteran news anchor Dan Avey. When KABC canceled Minyard and Tilden, it brought on Mark Germain ("Mr. KABC") for a period of time. Then it hired KFI's afternoon duo John and Ken to try to appeal to younger listeners but the show did not last. Soon followed the tandem of Dave Williams and Amy Lewis who broadcast live the events of 9/11.

When Ken returned with Avey, he strived to do a radio show that hearkened back to his past radio success: true talk radio without a contrived political agenda, mixed with humor. A September 1, 2003 article noted: "He's no conservative. He's not liberal either. Not even a libertarian, near as I can tell. He's kind of middle- of-the- road."

This observation by the author of the article, Steve Young, tells it all. Ken actually held a decidedly liberal viewpoint. But he did not let it direct the show. Young observed: "He doesn't seem to want to demean any party or ideology, except perhaps for the doom and gloomers. Still he seems pretty bright, has a decent sense of humor and on top of it is quite charming."

Unlike syndicated air mates Bill O' Reilly, Sean Hannity and Larry Elder, Minyard and Company did not have a conservative tilt. Rather, it followed the path of talk radio from a different era. Rather than shouting at listeners who disagreed with his views, like the conservative wave of talk radio show hosts, Minyard "does things like letting listeners finish sentences," Young observed. "Even when the caller says something Minyard disagrees with, he waits until they complete their thoughts before he comments."

Minyard calls this era and the current era as the "Foxification" of talk radio. We no longer have a venue for competing views. By the early 2000's the entire landscape of talk radio had changed. Callers who disagreed with the conservative host's views were "stupid," "misinformed" or had not done their research. Minyard did not demean his listeners and callers in that fashion. Rather, even in this last incarnation of his show, Minyard calmly ended each show with "EGBOK," everything's gonna be ok."

The Minyard and Company show from 2001-2004 provided Ken his chance of redeeming what he felt had been failures prior to his initial departure. Ken admitted to secretly tape recording various meetings with then KABC General Manager Drew Hayes, before his contract was not renewed for 1999. At the time he had no clue what direction KABC provided, or what it wanted to do with his show. This time, Ken got his free reign to run his show with his version of talk radio.

Speaking about his return to morning drive, Minyard said "KABC was my home for so many years, and I have fantastic memories. I'm excited to regain my friends both on and off the air in the morning." Partner Avey commented: "Working with Ken is a dream come true. We've been friends for years, and I think that will be obvious when people hear us on the air." KABC programmer Eric Braverman said that Avey would be a perfect complement to Minyard. "Dan's one of the most respected and credible voices in Southern California having countless awards over the years." Braverman touted the new show stating that Avey's sense of humor would be heightened by Minyard.

The show returned to the news/ humor format that was so successful for the Ken and Bob Company and Ken and Barkley. But the show did not shy away from politics. In a show on August 26, 2003, Los Angeles Police Chief William Bratton was interviewed about Special Order 40, which restricted police officers from asking individuals pulled over in their cars about their immigration status. Caller Steve stated: "The rest of your arguments are humorous. They're here illegally and his job is to uphold the law." Chief Bratton replied: "In as much as California has pretty much indicated that they don't want us involved in that issue, we're out of that business. If you don't like it leave the state."

Executive Producer of the show Terri West recalls Minyard as easy to work with but demanding." She produced many shows on KABC but describes Ken as her "favorite host" and compassionate. West, an African American, appreciated Minyard's addressing "topics such as racism, illegal immigration, gender-bias, the LGBT community and more." According to West, "Ken was a staunch supporter of immigrants and came to the defense of Latinos who tried to make a life in the United States." Minyard "kept his nose in the news and was always prepared. West would feed him news stories of the day, and "sometimes he would discuss them and sometimes he wouldn't. Hey, it was his show and he was the master of the domain. He was open-minded and welcomed any suggestions."

West also does not downplay Dan Avey's role on Ken and Company. According to West Avey "had a goofy sense of humor" and as the show progressed "lightened up." A newsman, Avey evolved into a willing and able sidekick to Minyard.

By 2001-2004, however, times at KABC had changed. The show had no budget. So no more travel with listeners or remote stunts. This frustrated Ken, leaving West to believe he retired early out of frustration. His ratings still frequently outpaced the rival KFI morning show with Bill Handel, who got his start as a contributor on Ken's show.

Still, Ken did not shy away from dealing with issues that conservatives pushed to the back burner. West did live interviews from Los Angeles' MacArthur park with Latinos when Matricular Consular cards were a hot topic. West interviewed undocumented immigrants on the air who Ken emphasized were day laborers just trying to feed their families.

The show had a nice run, but when Minyard turned 65, he opted for retirement. Ken had a say on his replacement. For a number of years, Doug McIntyre had done the overnight show called "Red Eye Radio" from 12:00 a.m. to 5:00 a.m. As McIntyre noted, he would "hand off" the show to Ken. Ken took a liking to Doug, and they began a daily segment at 5:45 a.m. at Blinky's Donuts with Doug offering irreverent thoughts: As Doug joked in an interview: "I gained 10 pounds doing those segments."

In a 2005 interview, Don Barrett interviewed Ken for LA Radio magazine. When Ken returned in 2001, he had a five-year contract. Three years into the five year contract, Ken elected to end his radio career. Ken told Barrett: "I didn't want to work forever, so I'd been planning at some point to do it… After five years, I was probably going to hang up radio anyway… But the whole thing was starting to get to me. There was the drive, the getting up at 2:30 a.m. It was just oppressive." Living in Oxnard, California in a home with a view of the water, along with his boat, meant for a very nice way of living. But the drive back from the show at 9:00 a.m. was unpleasant: "After you finished work and you're driving the 1 ½ hours back home, it's a bitch. My life has been saved any number of times by those dots in the middle of the road."

In September 2004, Ken decided to talk to management about his early retirement. Ken spoke with then President/ General Manager John Davison who handled the situation extremely well. Ken told Barrett: "I wrote John Davison a note saying how great they were with the way they handled the whole thing and I have absolutely no complaints about the way they treated me there. Having said that, I was really a fish out of the water with the current all-right-all- time version of KABC."

Reflecting on the changes in the radio business from the time he started to the time he called it quits, Ken told Barrett:

> "It's just not what it was –not as much fun. Talk radio in particular, is dulling sameness everywhere. For instance, in L.A. you've got KFI, KABC, KRLA, all shouting the same things about the same subjects, and now you have the liberal side with Air America. I think Air America will do very well in L.A. but their vision is

to simply do a left version of what the right is doing. I guess that makes a certain amount of sense in that they will have that side all to themselves and let the other three fight it out on the right. What Talk Radio once was about is what KGO in San Francisco is doing in San Francisco today."

Ken referred to talk radio as "the right wing echo chamber."

During the interview, Ken credited program director Eric Braverman for his hands off approach and that he did not ask Ken to change his liberal leaning views to "compromise my real beliefs to assuage management." In fact, Ken's shows different radically from those of the vocal conserve such as Rush Limbaugh, Sean Hannity, Mark Levin and Larry Elder:

"I came to an age in an era and with a belief that you should strive for civility and fairness on the radio.

Look how that has changed. I think it goes right back to the change in the Fairness Doctrine and equal time provisions... I never saw anything wrong with The Fairness Doctrine. Why shouldn't we have a requirement for balance on the publicly owned and regulated airwaves. Back when they had those restrictions, you couldn't have had what we have today on the radio and the public would be better for it."

When Ken referred to the Fairness Doctrine, he meant an FCC rule that radio stations putting on liberal views needed to give equal time on the air to conservative views and vice versa. Contrary to Ken's view, some have criticized the Fairness Doctrine for stifling political viewpoints and providing for bland radio. But anyone who listened to the Ken and Bob Company would realize that the Fairness Doctrine provided for much more interesting radio than what we currently have.

In any event, when Ken decided to retire in 2004, KABC finally gave him a proper send off with a retirement party at the Ritz Carlton hotel in Marina Del Rey, overlooking the water.

CHAPTER 8

THE RETIREMENT PARTY

When Ken Minyard began doing Talk Radio at KABC, Richard Nixon was President, the only X-rated film to win an Oscar, Midnight Cowboy won the Academy Award for Best Picture, construction on Walt Disney world began in Florida and two new passenger jets, the Boeing 747 and the Concord, flew their first flights. Neil Armstrong landed on the moon, and upstate New York witnessed the Woodstock festival. The upstart Miracle New York Mets won the World Series, and the New York Knicks with Walt "Clyde" Frazier, Willis Reed, Bill Bradley and Dave DeBusschere won their first NBA Championship.

Between 1969 and 2004, Minyard transformed talk radio. Minyard got his break when KABC teamed him up with veteran newsman Bob Arthur in 1973 for the 5- 9 a.m. morning drive. As the show evolved "we took what had been essentially been a news program and turned it into a news and entertainment show combination that really hadn't been done before," Minyard said in an interview with Al Peters in Radio and Records Magazine shortly after Minyard's retirement.

Minyard's final broadcast at the Marina del Rey Ritz Carlton hotel attracted not only many of his former ensemble members but other radio hosts such as KFI's morning host Bill Handel, who was a contributor on Minyard's show before he began his still continuing show in 1973.

Terri West, the Executive Producer of Ken and Company, recalls the retirement party:

> "The day of the party at the Ritz Carlton Marina del Rey was a quickly put-together production as the Programming department led the charge. As Executive Producer, I was thrown into a lion's den of hurried production, making phone calls to show guests who were Ken's radio circle dating years back. The most challenging part for a producer is the show clock. With a live remote production, anything could go wrong, but it didn't. That is, making sure that we came back from

commercial breaks on time, that the live audience cheered and applauded, that the audience questions were brief, etc. It was basically a fond farewell from Ken's longtime fans and colleagues. I recall Ken's successor, Doug McIntyre, off to the side in support to Ken's final show. I can't recall all of the show guests. There were a variety of call-ins from former co-hosts and other radio personalities.

Shelley Wagner, the director of the Marketing Department KABC, did the nuts bolts of putting together the retirement party. She set up the event at Ritz Carlton in Marina del Rey and made sure that breakfast was served for all who attended. It was a free event and an extremely large room was reserved. Wagner recalls that many of Ken's loyal listeners were invited to call in, and also that former members of the Ensemble such as Ciji Ware and Tommy Hawkins spoke at the party which was broadcast live on the air. After being contacted about this book, Don Barrett did an article on his website

Laradio.com on October 15, 2017 recalling the thirteen year anniversary of Ken's retirement party on October 15, 2004. With a line forming at 3 a.m. in the lobby of the Marina del Rey Ritz Carlton hotel on that Friday morning, a well-mannered group came to tribute Minyard's thirty years with KABC. Minyard opened up the show after the 5 am news officially for the last time. "I will see 2:30 a.m. this and no more," Ken quipped. Many of the warm memories came from the cast of professionals and characters on the Saturday Ken and Bob show. Barbara Esensten remembered her first broadcast was done naked in a hot tub. Barrett quoted her: "I could've electrocuted myself. My husband said I didn't actually have to do it naked but I knew Ken would know if I didn't." ABC and CNN anchor Aaron Brown called Ken his mentor for his years as an intern at the station. PBS host Tavis Smiley also appeared on the stage with Ken. Smiley told the audience: "You discovered me, and it's always dawned to me how all of this started."

From 1986-1995, Stu Nahan dispensed sports on the KABC morning show. Ken described Stu as "one of a kind." Stu told the story about the bachelor party that Ken threw for him a couple of days before his marriage. "It was held at a well-known restaurant on the West side, "Stu recalled Ken invited a lady who soon divested herself of her clothing. Ken took pictures of this lady standing next to me. On the day of the wedding, he walked up to my wife and gave her the pictures."

Ken's former partner Peter Tilden, then doing mornings at KZLA called in. The joke has always been that all of Ken's previous partners die. When Peter went in for a death threatening surgery a few years before the retirement party, he remembered, " I had a lot of people care about me, but none more than Ken. He wrote me a card, please don't die, it would look bad for me." It was while Ken and Peter were teamed together that the Hilary Clinton lesbian story surfaced. "We had Dick Morris on the air and he said it at out nowhere," remembered Ken. "He blew himself out of the water with the Clintons. That did it.

He blamed it on us, but we had it on tape. We played it over and over again."

Politicians and city officials called throughout the morning of the retirement party. Congressman David Drier, who was a Republican and Ken a Democrat, hoped that Ken's son Rick Minyard would be able to educate him about changing party affiliation. Police Chief William Bratton and Mayor James Hahn called in as well. The Mayor called Ken, "the ultimate radio personality in Los Angeles."

During the Ken and Bob Company era, Ken created a skit involving listener "weather watchers." One of them called in. Since the weather rarely changes much in Los Angeles, Ken distributed "Weather Watch Sticks" to various parts of the city. "You stick the stick out of the window and if it gets wet it is raining. If it was dry, it wasn't raining," explained Ken.

Barrett wrote on his website that Lonnie Lardner used to do the news on the morning show. "I'd always prepare my segments with you and then you would throw out something that would make me reveal personal aspects of my life that I couldn't do with anyone else," Lonnie told Ken. "I'm now going to save on therapy sessions," she confessed. Lonnie stayed in the hotel Thursday before the show and admitted she indulged in a number of adult beverages. "My head was hurting and I knew it would be the sleep of death. I wake up this morning and turn on the radio and hear Bob Arthur and thought I had died. I figured that Ken finally killed me." It was a 1986 air segment replayed that she heard.

Michael Reagan thanked Ken for his radio career. "You've always given our family a fair shake," Michael said by phone. "Ron Reagan and I talked more since June than we've ever talked before." Reagan admitted that his family has always been different politically. "I've got a family just like that," quipped Ken.

Tommy Hawkins, former NBA star and then with the Dodger organization, said that working the morning show from 1970 to 1985 was the best job of his broadcast career. "It was incredible. When Ken wanted to loosen up the very buttoned –down Bob Arthur he had Tommy bring in a model who would take her top off. We hid her in the bathroom and when Bob started a newscast she came into the studio and put her bodacious ta-ta's on Bob's shoulders. And Bob kept reading. He was imperturbable. It was Edie Williams of Russ Myers films. She was ticked off and ran over and sat on Ken's lap and rigor mortis sat in with Ken and he couldn't move. He couldn't push the microphone button. He was frozen," said Hawkins.

Near the end of the show, Steve Edwards, who frequently appeared as a guest on Ken's shows, ran a live shot on his good day LA TV program on Fox Channel 11. Steve introduced Ken as "the voice and face of morning radio in LA for thirty five years." During the retirement party, Ken played a portion of the drunk/ hangover show. Steve was working at KBC at the time and called in "Ken, I know you're late and I know you feel bad. I want you to know you really handled that badly." When the live shot ended, Ken told his audience that Steve did a great radio show. "It's the only show that I was moved to call into."

Ken's successor Doug McIntyre said on the show, "this is a sad day for radio but a hell of a day for the wine merchants of Oxnard." Doug was mentioning Ken's retirement home on the water in Oxnard, California. Doug talked about the KABC building built largely because of Ken. "The facility on La Cienega is one the great stations- a great legacy station and much of the credit goes to the success that Ken brought to morning drive. The Red Sox had 3 left fielders- Ted Williams, Carl Yastrzemski, and Jim Rice for over forty-five years. KABC has had one morning show for the greatest part of its history. I am deeply moved and humbled to take a shot at it." Reminiscing about Ken in an interview in September 2017, McInyre recalled that Ken would often come to work "over nourished" meaning that Ken could drink with the best of them. His wife Jaqi told me they definitely "partied" and had a good time. But, it seems, always in the spirit of EGBOK.

In his interview with Barrett, Ken imparted his philosophy on life. "I've always liked to work hard and play hard. The balance would tip towards play. When Bob and I came together it occurred the best to make it happen was to make work into play. And it has been for most of the time. And surround yourself with great people."

By the time Minyard retired, however, he had soured on Talk Radio. Asked by Barrett how he felt about Talk Radio, Minyard remarked:

> "Honestly, there is not a lot I like about it today. I don't really like how so much of it has become a propaganda machine. And I lament that there is not more balanced discussion on what are, after all, the public airwaves. I also think that things like

syndication have added to the demise of a lot of local programming, and I have always felt that localism was radio's biggest strength."

What Minyard commented back in 2004 he now dubs "The Foxication of Talk Radio." During the heyday of the Ken and Bob Company, Minyard had created a listener friendly program filled with a human touch along the way. But by 2004, Talk Radio had turned decidedly conservative. Anyone in disagreement with the host often would get yelled at and hung up on. Minyard swears that since his retirement in October 2004, he has not listened to KABC, or any broadcast radio, again.

But through social media, Minyard continues to be heard loud and clear.

Ken and Rick Minyard

Traffic reporter and daily contributor Jorge Jarrin with sports commentator Stu Nahan.

Doug McIntyre, who succeeded Ken in 2004 on KABC's morning drive, along with Rob Marinko, who did the news on the show and provided an interview for this book.

CHAPTER 9
BEYOND KABC

When Ken Minyard announced his retirement in 2004, few of his listeners believed that he would stay off the air forever. Still extremely vital and only 65, it seemed that Ken had more to say. Perhaps a weekend show where he could focus on news and politics, some wondered. But Minyard meant it. He had enough of radio, and particularly KABC. He has not listened to KABC since the day he retired in 2004.

Ken did not go back on the air, as many predicted following his retirement. But he continued to have a voice. Not simply content to retire in Oxnard with his boat, Ken became visibly politically active, particularly on social media. Even with this forum, friends like Leon Kaplan tried to coax him to do interviews on his popular Sunday "Motorman" show but Ken declined. Minyard meant it when he retired: he simply had enough of AM radio. Kaplan at one time appeared on KABC seven days a week: in the 7-9 p.m. slot during the week, on the Ken and Bob Saturday Special and on his Sunday show. Still in his morning Sunday slot, Kaplan states that once his show ends, he cannot wait for the next week's show. By the time Ken retired, Kaplan felt that Ken viewed it as a job and it was not fun for him anymore.

He did just view it as a job. And he did not want to dial it in, instead going out on top. Interestingly, given Minyard's dominant personality on the radio for years, he has shied away from newspaper interviews and other media appearances since his retirement.

Part of this, of course, stemmed from discord occurring on KABC during his close to 30 year run. The bitterness with Bob "retiring" was far surpassed by the antipathy Roger Barkley and his friends displayed when Ken actually fought for Barkley's job and got him another year. Being told not to go to Barkley's funeral particularly stung. The mismatch with Tilden did not help matters and of course the station's decision not to renew his seven figure contract left a sour taste in his mouth.

Even more than these personal dramas, Ken just disdained the path KABC and talk radio took. The demise of the Fairness Doctrine and "Foxification" of talk radio caused Ken to truly despise AM radio and fueled his later political efforts.

In a free-ranging interview with Minyard in August 2016, he related his view that Barack Obama was one of our best presidents ever. Minyard began posting on Facebook in the fall 2009. His son Rick stated that "Ken began doing his show on Facebook." At first, his posts took the route of many of ours. The posts talked about family and other personal matters. Soon, though, Minyard let go of the constraints he had while a morning radio host and let his political views known. As early as November 2009, Minyard posted: "Anyone notice that Rush Limbaugh has a fixation on the anus? Minyard quoted Limbaugh as stating Obama "knows he's being followed around by a bunch of sycophants who are going to die of anal poisoning."

While over the top, this type of post gave a preview of Minyard's eventual assault on the politics of Donald Trump.

Minyard's legacy did not go unnoticed. In a January 10, 2010 post from Conservative radio personality Rob Marinko, he wrote:

> "Hey Ken, it's been too long. I hope you and yours are well. Holy crap everything's changed since you left. Yep, I know you're fully aware of the sinking ship on La Cienega. Please take this only as a compliment that it is meant to be. Wow- that does not sound as good as I had hoped. Thanks again for all the neat things I was able to learn from you. I just wish I had more time to put them into practice. Anyway, take good care."

Marinko plainly liked the time that he spent with Minyard despite their divergent political views.

Ken remained an ardent supporter of Obama throughout his remainder of the presidency in 2016. However, beginning in 2015 and continuing through 2016, Ken became ever more vocal on social media regarding his disdain for Trump and his support for Clinton. If I recounted every Facebook post here, this book would go on for miles. I will summarize some of the most important ones in my view. Minyard hit the main issue on the head in a May 6, 2016 post about the next Supreme Court Justice after the death of Antonin Scalia. Minyard wrote on May 16, 2016: "This perhaps is the most important and least talked issue in the campaign for both Republicans and Democrats. The next President will serve a maximum of eight years. The next Supreme Court Justice could serve decades. The choice is clear. If you want a justice that will be like the late Antonin Scalia then that is what Republicans will offer. To refer a more progressive choice then you should vote for the Democrat."

Minyard, like many, felt emboldened by the early census counts regarding the Clinton/ Trump campaign. Those campaign tallies maintained through the late election year. On October 30, 2016, Minyard posted: "Clinton leading Trump by 15% among early voters. These were absentee ballots, not an indicator about how the election would turn, but important information."

Minyard remained relentless on Trump during the entire campaign. On October 12, 2016, he posted that "six women and counting have now accused Donald Trump of the inappropriate behavior similar to that which he bragged about to Billy Bush. Beauty contestants say he walked in on them while they were nude. And one lady charged him with rape. The Trump campaign denied everything and said the accusations are invalid and unsubstantiated."

It makes no sense to recount all of Minyard's posts about Trump here. The point is Minyard fervently opposed the Trump campaign. He pointed out, cogently, a number of things about Trump that were disturbing. He noted the Supreme Court appointment issue. He raised frequently Trump flip- flopping on numerous issues, such as tax reform and illegal immigration. Indeed, as described earlier, Minyard always held a strong stance in support of immigrants. As his wife Jaqi told me in an interview: "He married a Mexican so he understands."

Trump, of course, got elected in November 2016. This disheartened Minyard, and he kept his vigil against Trump, noting all of his missteps. To this day, Minyard on his Facebook page, and on a page with his son called Minyard and Minyard, continue to denounce Trump on most of his initiatives.

Minyard has commented on almost every subject regarding Trump. On Trump's war with the FBI, in view of the special prosecutor's pardon of Flynn among other things, Minyard noted his inconsistent positions:

> "After Trump slammed the FBI for being in tatters and the worst shape in history he then makes a speech saying anti-police sentiment is wrong. Is it possible he

doesn't realize that the FBI is the largest law enforcement agency in the country?"

Ken also developed a Facebook group with his son Rick called Minyard and Minyard. In a recent post, covering all the topics they both despised about Trump, they wrote:

"Hey Trump and Republicans:
- You've tried to screw with our healthcare.
- You've assaulted our educational system.
- You've destroyed our image overseas.
- You lie about things that can be disproven with our own eyes and ears in real time.
- You're messing with our tax system that has done pretty damn well for the economy in the past 9 years.
- You've unleashed the power of women onto the world.
- You taint the legal system and law enforcement agencies.

- You coddle and accept racists into your movement, and you have encouraged violence against us.
- You've invited a foreign power into our elections and continue to suck up to it while attacking those that we have tasked to expose the trouble.
- We have noticed: you're standing among all but a small, uneducated, aging base is just about as low as it can get. And now you've gone and fucked with our internet, despite 80+% of us who told you NOT to. Brilliant move. You have unleashed a vast army of 20-somethings who have, to this point, not paid attention to this stuff. No longer, we will make sure they know who has done this, and how they go about fixing it by simply <u>voting</u>. You are headed for a historic ass-kicking in 2018. And so long as you keep confined to your bubble with your rallies, and your media, you'll never see it coming. What you have seen so far is mere child's play

compared to what next year will bring. You lost a Senate seat in Alabama this week. In ALABAMA!
- Happy Holidays."

For years, Minyard was silenced, to some extent, on talk radio. Now, he has an open voice. Reading his and his son Rick's Facebook sites yields considerably important information. While some are inflammatory most hit the mark. With no doubt, Ken and Rick will continue to have his voice heard, well past his thirty-one year run in talk radio.

Ken, Rick, Kevin and Dana Minyard prior to Kevin's passing.

Jaqi and Ken

Postscript

To say this book did not go as expected would understate. Once Ken embraced my idea in August 2016, we envisioned many meetings where Ken could review each draft and regale me with other stories. But Ken lost his son Kevin to cancer in November 2016 and at at virtually the same time, got diagnosed with cancer himself. After a yearlong struggle when Ken could not meet with me in person because of his illness and treatment, Ken got the news that the cancer had spread, and a longer struggle lay ahead.

During that time, I lost my father on April 23, 2017 at 2:58 a.m. after a long battle with the vicious Alzheimer's disease. Ken's illness and my dad's death stalled this book.

Then the unfathomable happened. At almost exactly 2:58 a.m. in the morning of August 6, 2017, my wife Cathy and I learned that our son Jake at 21 had died of an overdose. The ensuing months, filled with such profound sadness in our family, with his surviving sisters

Nicole and Jordan (Jake's twin) made it impossible for me to continue writing.

But determined, I turned back to the book and hope I have adequately chronicled Ken's amazing career and persona. While I am sure this book would have been longer had Ken not fallen ill, we all feel the book tells the story almost fully.

What I have learned the most through all of this is how the Minyard's, as well as my family, have come together in adversity. So when I started this I did not know I had anything in common with a radio icon, I now know our love of family, and our family's love of us, created a bond between us that I will treasure forever.

Craig A. Horowitz has practiced employment law for 31 years. He also has written two prior published books "Row 47" and "The Legislative Legacy of Edward M. Kennedy." Craig and his family live in Santa Monica, California.

Made in the USA
San Bernardino, CA
15 January 2018